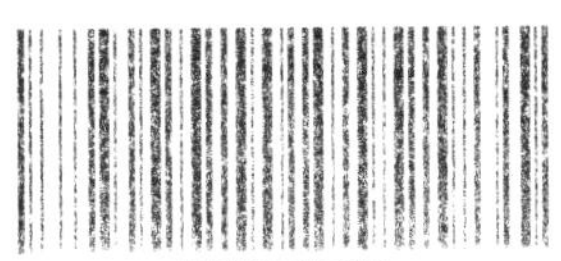

Research It!

The Industrial Revolution

Neil Morris

Raintree

www.raintreepublishers.co.uk
Visit our website to find out more information about Raintree books.

To order:
Phone 0845 6044371
Fax +44 (0) 1865 312263
Email myorders@raintreepublishers.co.uk

Customers from outside the UK please telephone +44 1865 312262

Raintree is an imprint of Capstone Global Library Limited, a company incorporated in England and Wales having its registered office at 7 Pilgrim Street, London, EC4V 6LB - Registered company number: 6695582.

Edited by Andrew Farrow and Rebecca Vickers
Designed by Steven Mead
Picture research by Ruth Blair
Production by Victoria Fitzgerald
Originated by Capstone Global Library Ltd
Printed and bound in China by South China Printing Company Ltd

ISBN 978 0 431 11616 7 (hardback)
14 13 12 11 10
10 9 8 7 6 5 4 3 2 1

ISBN 978 0 431 11623 5 (paperback)
14 13 12 11 10
10 9 8 7 6 5 4 3 2 1

British Library Cataloguing in Publication Data
Morris, Neil, 1946-
The Industrial Revolution. -- (Research it!)
1. Industrial revolution--Research--Methodology--Juvenile literature.
I. Title II. Series
909.8'1'072-dc22

Acknowledgements
We would like to thank the following for permission to reproduce photographs: Alamy: pp. **6** (© Robert Morris), **10** (© Philip Scalia), **32** (© Vintage Images); Corbis: pp. **5**, **38**, **42**, **45**, (Bettmann), **50**, (moodboard), **36**; Getty Images: pp. **9**, **11**, **25**, **40**, **46** (Hulton Archive), **17** (Time & Life Pictures); ©iStockphoto: p. **37** (© Clifford Mueller); ©Rex Features: p. **41**; Shutterstock: p. **27** (© Marc Dietrich); ©Shutterstock and ©iStockphoto: design features and backgrounds.

The main cover image of a vintage steam engine is reproduced with permission of shutterstock/©SF Photo. The background images are reproduced with permission of the following: iStockphoto (©Olena Druzhynina, ©Boros Emese, ©Bill Noll, ©Dieter Spears) and shutterstock (©Lars Lindblad, ©Nik Niklz, ©Picsfive).

We would like to thank Stewart Ross for his invaluable help in the preparation of this book.

Every effort has been made to contact copyright holders of material reproduced in this book. Any omissions will be rectified in subsequent printings if notice is given to the publishers.

Contents

Some words are printed in bold, **like this**. You can find out what they mean by looking in the glossary.

What Is Research?

The word *research* can be a noun or a verb. It comes from the French *rechercher*, meaning "search closely" or "investigate thoroughly". When you research a subject, you study sources carefully to investigate it in detail. Research allows you to study evidence and establish facts. You can then reach conclusions about the subject you are investigating.

Looking at history

History is the study of past events. The Industrial Revolution happened because of a series of events that started hundreds of years ago. Present-day historians have done their own research into the events that made up the Industrial Revolution. Historians study records of these events which helps them to answer important questions. Their questions about the past give focus and direction to their research, leading them to sources that provide evidence for certain answers. In this way, researchers' questions help them to build a picture of the past.

Asking questions

You may want to research the Industrial Revolution because you have been given a project that asks a question related to it. This might be a broad question, such as "What was the Industrial Revolution?". If that is the case, you will need to break down the question into narrower, more manageable questions about various aspects of the Industrial Revolution. For ways that you can narrow a topic, see pages 22–25.

If you are doing your own research, rather than answering a question as a project, you will still want to ask useful, relevant questions about the topic. They will lead you to the kind of evidence that will provide answers. Here are some examples of good questions:

- How did iron-making improve during the Industrial Revolution?
- What was new about factories in the Industrial Revolution?
- Why was steam power so important?
- Why did people build canals?
- What were working conditions in factories like as the Industrial Revolution developed?
- When did trade unions become recognized?
- Did the development of a railway system affect the Industrial Revolution?

This engraving from the 1870s is a primary source. It shows men loading an iron-smelting furnace with ore. Iron was vitally important to the Industrial Revolution.

Two kinds of sources

Historians look for evidence in their research to help them answer questions. The places where they find evidence are called sources. There are two kinds of sources.

- **Primary sources**
  Scholars and authors of history books often use **primary sources**. These are first-hand sources that come from the period being studied and were created at the time. Primary sources include written documents, such as official records kept by government institutions, schools and universities, churches, industrial companies, and trade unions. They may also include legal and military records and birth, marriage, and death certificates. Diaries, letters, and family documents are also primary sources. Novels, poetry, and other literary writings from the time can provide background information and add colour to a particular period and location. Any form of illustration, such as paintings and photographs, can also be extremely valuable primary source research tools. **Artefacts**, such as equipment and clothing from the time, are also primary sources.
- **Secondary sources**
  Works written later about the period in question are called **secondary sources**. Many of your sources will be secondary. Books (such as encyclopedias and **atlases**) and websites about the Industrial Revolution are secondary sources, though they may quote from or refer to primary sources. You can consult secondary sources and use them to put together your own answers to questions. Every person's research is original and will be slightly different from anyone else's.

Overview of the Subject

When researching the Industrial Revolution, the first questions to ask must include:

- *What* was the Industrial Revolution?
- *When and where* did the Industrial Revolution take place?

What ... ?

The best place to look for quick definitions is in a **reference** book, such as a dictionary. The *New Oxford Dictionary* defines the Industrial Revolution as:

"The rapid development of industry that occurred in Britain in the late 18th and early 19th centuries, brought about by the introduction of machinery. It was characterized by the use of steam power, the growth of factories, and the mass production of manufactured goods."

This definition makes it clear that, in this context, the word *revolution* means "rapid development". A definition for the word *revolution* in the dictionary is "a dramatic and wide-reaching change in the way something works or is organized". In this case, the "something" is industry. The word *industry* is separately defined as "economic activity concerned with the processing of raw materials and manufacture of goods in factories".

The world's first successful water-powered cotton-spinning mill was opened by Richard Arkwright in 1771 near Matlock, Derbyshire. Today the mill is owned by the Arkwright Society and is a valuable resource for visiting researchers.

Another place to look for definitions is an **encyclopedia**. *World Book Encyclopedia* points out: "The term *Industrial Revolution* refers both to the changes that occurred and to the period itself." This is an important point, and you will notice that many sources use phrases such as "during the Industrial Revolution", meaning during that period.

When ... ?

The Industrial Revolution is not as easy to define as events such as a war or a period of office. World War I took place between 1914 and 1918, and George Washington served as the first president of the United States from 1789 to 1797. All sources agree on these dates. But not all sources will agree on the dates of the Industrial Revolution. According to *Encyclopaedia Britannica* the term Industrial Revolution was not used until the 19th century.

Encyclopaedia Britannica gives a precise date (1760) as the beginning of the Industrial Revolution, while other sources suggest earlier or later dates. The earliest date you could quote would probably be 1709, when the English iron-maker Abraham Darby converted a furnace to smelt iron with **coke** instead of charcoal. From that point, coke gradually replaced charcoal as the best fuel for iron making, and this new process was an important feature of the Industrial Revolution.

Many sources state that the Industrial Revolution began "in the 18th century". Your research will probably include more specific dates that you can include if the information is relevant to your specific question. In this book, the examples are taken mainly from the earlier years of the Industrial Revolution, as they are so important to an understanding of the whole period.

... and where?

All sources agree that the Industrial Revolution began in England. In 18th-century Britain, conditions were right for a change from an agricultural to an industrial society. The country had large deposits of coal and iron that were essential for the energy and material needs of industrialization. Britain was a successful colonial and trading power. Its **colonies** produced raw materials and became markets for manufactured goods. Before the existence of factories, textiles and other goods were made in rural homes and small workshops. **Cottage industry** overlapped with the factory system that began in 1771, when Richard Arkwright opened a water-powered mill in Derbyshire (see page 6). The new factory system gradually and **sporadically** spread across Britain.

Spreading around Europe

Beginning at the end of the 18th century, new technology and manufacturing methods spread from Britain to the continent of Europe. In 1799, the English inventor William Cockerill (1759–1832) set up wool-spinning machines near Liège, in what was then France and is now Belgium. Early in the 19th century, industry developed fast in this region. Coal mines were updated with conveyor belts that increased production, and iron and steel production developed. By the middle of the century France had joined Britain as an industrial power.

In Germany, growing railways led to an increase in demand for coal and iron, and industrial centres in the north of Germany expanded. Historical events, such as Prussia's victory over France, and German unification in 1871, set the stage for the foundation of large, successful companies. German scientists, inventors, and industrialists helped their country dominate the new chemical and electrical industries.

What really happened?

In your research you might come across some interesting stories that could be **apocryphal**. This means the particular story is widely held to be true, but experts may doubt its authenticity. It will be impossible for you to check the real truth, and even a professional historian might find that difficult. But you can use a phrase such as "there is a story that ..." or "some experts believe that ...".

A good example of this is from research into a fascinating story about James Hargreaves (c. 1720–78), who is widely held (notice the use of this phrase!) to be the inventor of the spinning jenny. This was the first practical device to wind **yarn** on to more than one spindle at the same time. Hargreaves **patented** his machine in 1770. The apocryphal bit, as described by *Encyclopaedia Britannica*, appears below in **italics**:

"About 1764 Hargreaves is said to have conceived the idea for his hand-powered multiple spinning machine when he observed a spinning wheel that had been accidentally overturned by his young daughter Jenny. As the spindle continued to revolve in an upright rather than a horizontal position, Hargreaves reasoned that many spindles could be so turned."

Grolier's *New Book of Knowledge* encyclopedia similarly uses words to indicate that the account may be apocryphal:

"One day in 1764, so the story goes, a clever Englishman named James Hargreaves (?– 1778) sat watching his daughter at her spinning wheel. As she stood up to rest from her work, the wheel accidentally tipped over and lay on its side. Hargreaves watched the wheel and spindle still turning. Like a flash, an idea came to him."

The underlining has been added to show you the type of phrase that can be used when it is not possible to prove that something is true. You could certainly put the story in your own words and add a similar phrase.

If you are interested in reading an alternative version of the story, visit the Cotton Times website (www.cottontimes.co.uk/hargreaveso.htm). The writer, Doug Peacock, does not believe that Hargreaves invented the spinning jenny at all, but that he simply improved on a machine that had been invented "by an obscure artisan called Thomas Highs, who was the true genius of the Industrial Revolution".

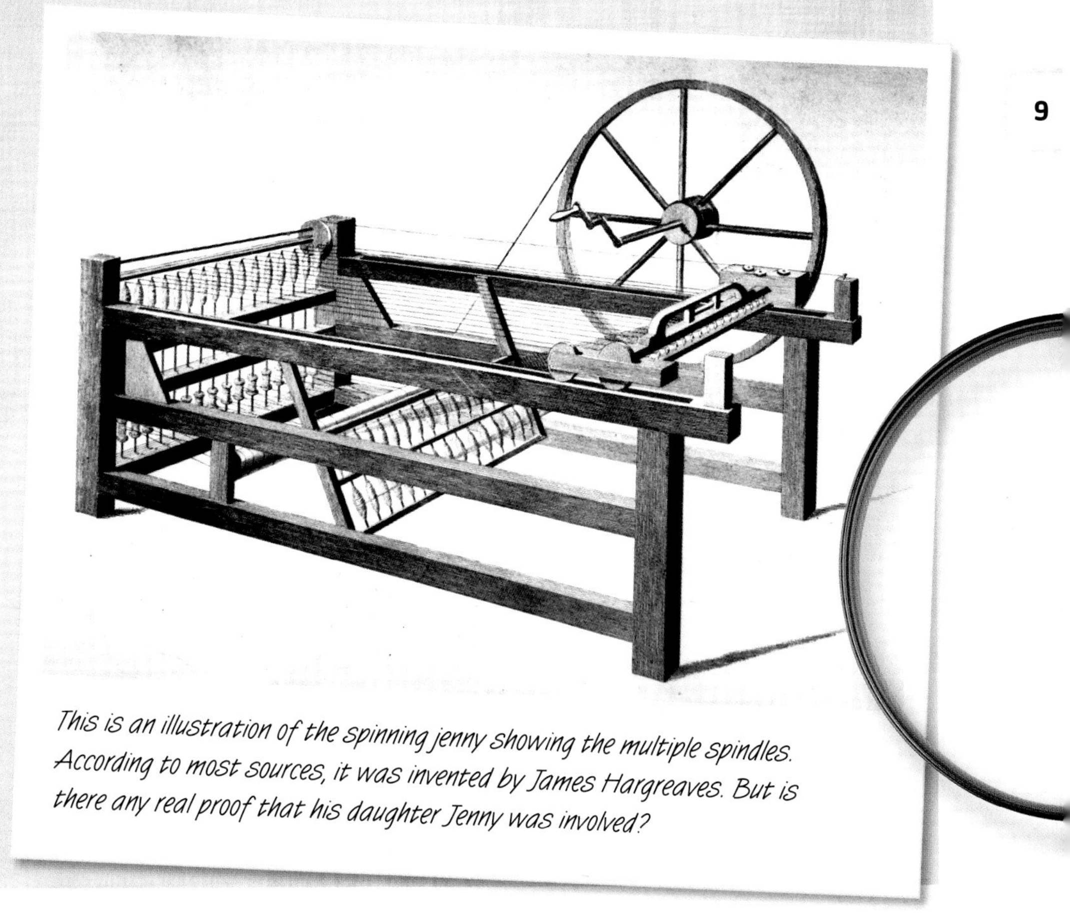

This is an illustration of the spinning jenny showing the multiple spindles. According to most sources, it was invented by James Hargreaves. But is there any real proof that his daughter Jenny was involved?

To the New World

The factory system was taken across the Atlantic by an English textile worker named Samuel Slater (1768–1835), who went to the United States in 1789. He left England in disguise because the British government did not allow anyone who knew about the design and operation of spinning machines to leave the country. However, Slater slipped the net and set up a factory of spinning machines in Pawtucket, Rhode Island.

The Lowell system

Another significant step towards the industrialization of the United States came in 1812, when the American textile industrialist Francis Cabot Lowell (1775–1817) founded the Boston Manufacturing Company in Waltham, Massachusetts (see page 36). He developed a system to manufacture textiles that other mills then used as a model.

This 21st-century photograph shows the 19th-century textile mills beside the Merrimack River in Lowell, Massachusetts, USA, the city named after Francis Cabot Lowell.

The armory system

In the early 19th century another important industrial development took place in the United States when the **small arms industry** developed machines that could produce standard parts. This "armory system" marked the beginning of mass production, and the idea soon spread to other industries, such as sewing and harvesting-machine manufacturers.

This photograph, dating from the early 1860s, shows the machine room for rifle barrels at the Remington Armory in New York state. When the American Civil War broke out, the U.S. government ordered 5,000 rifles, and the Armory started using steam power.

The transformation of the United States into an industrial nation gathered pace after the end of the American Civil War (1861–65) between the northern Union states and the southern Confederate states. Coal and steel production increased, and railways were built across the continent. Many more factories opened and industry advanced much faster than agriculture.

A second revolution

Some historians refer to developments in the United States as a second Industrial Revolution, after the first in Britain and parts of Europe. Others refer to the second Industrial Revolution as the use of electricity in industry, transport, and communications. *Encyclopaedia Britannica* says that a "new" Industrial Revolution started in the late 19th century:

"Despite considerable overlapping with the 'old,' there is mounting evidence for a 'new' Industrial Revolution in the late 19th and 20th centuries. In terms of basic materials, modern industry has begun to exploit many natural and synthetic resources not hitherto utilized: lighter metals, new ***alloys****, and synthetic products, such as plastics, as well as new energy sources."*

After doing your research, you can come to your own conclusions about a "second" or "new" Industrial Revolution. Once again, if in doubt, you can say that "some historians" call it that.

Timelines

Dates are important in any study of history, and a timeline can be useful both to help you in your research and to present facts in a report. A timeline can be a simple chart of dates or can be presented in a more detailed way, with dates spread across or down the page and events placed in the appropriate positions. A specialist timeline, such as one on Britain's first canals (below), can be looked at alongside a more general one covering many aspects of the Industrial Revolution and its impact on different places, such as the timeline on pages 12–14.

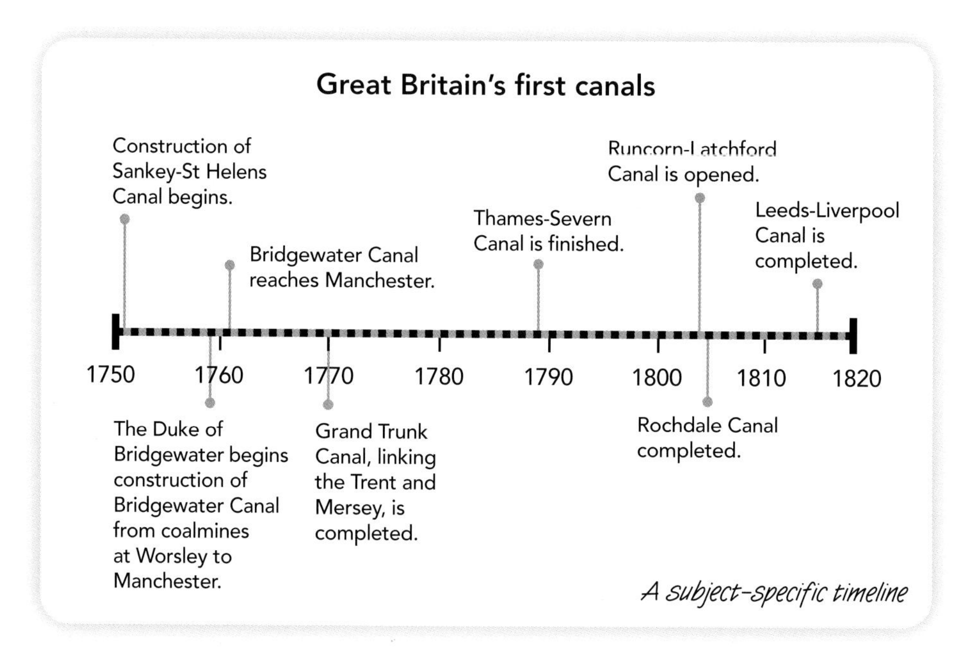

A subject-specific timeline

Timeline of the Industrial Revolution

Britain

1709	Abraham Darby (1678–1717) converts a furnace to smelt iron with coke instead of charcoal.
1712	Thomas Newcomen (1663–1729) builds the first commercially successful steam engine.
1733	John Kay (1704–64) develops the flying shuttle, which weaves yarn mechanically rather than by hand.
1761	The Bridgewater Canal links the coalmines of Worsley to Manchester.
1764	James Hargreaves (1722–78) invents the spinning jenny.
1769	Josiah Wedgwood (1730–95) opens a pottery-making factory near Stoke-on-Trent in Staffordshire. Richard Arkwright (1732–92) patents his water frame, a spinning machine powered by water. James Watt (1736–1819) develops an improved steam engine.

1771	Arkwright opens a water-powered mill in Cromford, Derbyshire.
1773	A group of brokers establishes a **stock exchange** in London.
1774	Matthew Boulton (1728–1809) and James Watt open a steam-engine factory in Birmingham.
1776	*An Inquiry into the Nature and Causes of the Wealth of Nations* by Adam Smith (1723–90) is published; Smith is the founder of modern economics.
1779	Samuel Crompton (1753–1827) develops the spinning mule, a cross between the spinning jenny and the water frame. The first steam-powered mills open.
1785	James Watt's steam engine is first used to power a cotton mill. Edmund Cartwright (1743–1823) patents his power loom.
1786	Scottish engineer Andrew Meikle (1719–1811) develops a water-powered **threshing machine**. Arkwright first uses a Watt engine in a cotton mill in Blackfriars, London.
1789	The Thames-Severn Canal links the two rivers.
1791	A Manchester mill orders 400 of Cartwright's power looms, but is burned down by workers fearing for their jobs.
1799	The new Combination Acts outlaw trade unions (**repealed** in 1824).
1801	Richard Trevithick (1771–1833) builds a steam carriage.
1804	Trevithick runs a steam locomotive on rails in an ironworks.
1806–59	Isambard Kingdom Brunel builds many railway lines and tunnels, bridges, and steamships during his lifetime.
1809	Parliament awards Cartwright £10,000 for the benefits to the nation of his power loom.
1811–16	During Luddite riots, workers destroy machines they fear will replace them.
1814	*The Times* newspaper is printed on a steam-driven press.
1816	The Leeds-Liverpool Canal is completed.
1823	English mathematician Charles Babbage (1791–1871) develops his difference engine, a mechanical computing machine.
1825	George Stephenson (1781–1848) builds the 40-km (25-mile) long Stockton & Darlington Railway.
1829	Stephenson's *Rocket* locomotive travels at 46 kph (29 mph).
1831	Michael Faraday (1791–1867) discovers the principle of electromagnetic induction, later used in electric generators.
1837	British inventor William Cooke (1806–79) and physicist Charles Wheatstone (1802–75) patent a **telegraph** device for use on railways.
1838	The Liverpool & Manchester Railway is extended south to London; there are now 800 km (500 miles) of railway track in Britain.
1840	Rowland Hill (1795–1879) introduces prepaid mail and the first postage stamps.
1851	The Great Exhibition opens on 1 May in Hyde Park, London, and runs until 11 October; more than 6 million people pay to visit the exhibition.
1855	Henry Bessemer (1813–98) **patents** his process for converting pig iron into steel.

1858	Launch of Brunel's *Great Eastern*, the largest ship built up to this time.
1866	The *Great Eastern* successfully lays a **telegraph** cable across the Atlantic.
1868	First meeting of the Trades Union Congress takes place, in Manchester.
1871	The Trade Union Act recognizes unions by law.
1889	The Great Dock Strike in London secures wage increases and overtime pay.
1901	Italian inventor Guglielmo Marconi (1874–1937) sends the first transatlantic signal, from Cornwall to Canada.

Belgium, France, and Germany

1801	French inventor Joseph-Marie Jacquard (1752–1834) develops a loom that can weave cloth with intricate patterns.
1827–32	The Charleroi–Brussels Canal is built.
1837	The first public railway in France opens between Paris and Saint Germain.
1869	Alfred Krupp introduces the open-hearth steelmaking process in his factory in Essen, Germany.
1870	Deutsche Bank is founded in Germany as a specialist bank for foreign trade.
1879	German Werner von Siemens (1816–92) builds the first electric railway.
1885	In Germany, Karl Benz (1844–1929) develops the first automobile to run on an internal combustion engine.

United States

1793	American inventor Eli Whitney (1765–1825) develops a cotton gin that separates seeds from fibres, speeding up production of the raw material.
1807	American engineer Robert Fulton (1765–1815) builds the first successful steamboat, the *Clermont*.
1819	The American-built *Savannah* is the first steamship to cross the Atlantic.
1839	Connecticut inventor Charles Goodyear discovers vulcanization, a process to make rubber stronger.
1844	Samuel Morse (1791–1872), inventor in 1838 of the Morse Code, builds a test telegraph line between Baltimore and Washington, D.C.
1851	Isaac Singer (1811–75) develops an improved sewing machine.
1859	Edwin Drake (1819–80) strikes oil near Titusville, Pennsylvania.
1869	Railway lines meet at Promontory, Utah, to complete the first continuous track across the country. The first U.S. national workers' organization, the Noble Order of the Knights of Labor, is founded in Philadelphia.
1876	Alexander Graham Bell (1847–1922) displays his telephone at Philadelphia's Centennial Exhibition.
1879	Thomas Edison invents the light bulb.
1903	The Wright brothers, Wilbur (1867–1912) and Orville (1871–1948), make the first successful flight in a powered aircraft.
1913	Henry Ford (1863–1947) begins mass-producing the Model-T car.

Biographies

A biography is an account of a person's life. When researching historical subjects, you may find biographies useful. They can tell you a lot about the people who shaped events. Biographies of inventors, engineers, and builders can be useful in your research. The *Oxford Dictionary of National Biography (DNB)*, for example, is an illustrated collection of more than 56,600 biographies of the men and women from around the world who shaped the history of Britain. Each biography ends with a list of sources, **archives**, and photographs.

Most public libraries in the UK – and many in other parts of the world – subscribe to the *DNB*. Many of them offer "remote access", which means that you may be able to access the *DNB* **online** at home. Visit www.oxforddnb.com/public/index.html to access the *DNB* at home using your library membership.

Everyday lives

The study of history does not just involve people in positions of power, such as political leaders, or those who achieve great things in their lifetime, such as inventors. The social and economic changes brought about by the Industrial Revolution affected the lives of all men, women, and children. In Britain and elsewhere, there were great contrasts between the different classes of society during the 18th and 19th centuries. Life was especially difficult for poor people.

Of course, you will not find an article on a poor person in reference works. So how can you research poverty, say, or working conditions? You will have to use secondary sources and look up the themes in which you are interested. You might, for example, find material on conditions for the poor in London during Victorian times.

Some books may include descriptions of the lives of ordinary people. You must bear in mind, however, that life in London may have been quite different from life in the countryside or other British cities. You cannot draw general conclusions from one specific example, just as you would not assume that other educated, successful men lived in the same way as the great engineer Isambard Kingdom Brunel (see page 43).

Finding and Organizing Facts

When you approach a new Industrial Revolution topic, a **KWL chart** is a good way to get your thinking organized. A KWL chart is type of **graphic organizer**. KWL stands for "Know/Want to know/Learn":

- What do you already **K**now at the start of your research?
- What do you **W**ant to know?
- What have you **L**earned during your research?

To create a KWL chart, make a column for each of these three questions. You can fill in the first column with statements and the second with questions before you begin your research. You can fill in the third column as you work. A KWL chart helps you to make sure that you have enough facts to cover the topic or answer the particular question. It also helps you focus on what you need to find out as you do your research.

KWL chart

Topic: *Protest during the Industrial Revolution*
Question: *Who were the Luddites?*

What I **K**now	What I **W**ant to know	What I **L**earned
They were a group of machine breakers.	*Where did their name come from?*	*"Captain Ludd" probably never existed.*
They were active in England in the early 19th century.	*Why did they break machines? What did they hope to achieve?*	*They feared that new automated machines would mean the loss of jobs for skilled textile workers.*
		Some Luddites were executed and others were transported to Australia.

What really happened?

This is another opportunity for you to make up your own mind based on your research. On the etymology (origin) of the term Luddite, the *Oxford English Dictionary* says:
"According to Pellew's Life of Lord Sidmouth (1847) III. 80, Ned Lud was a person of weak intellect who lived in a Leicestershire village about 1779, and who in a fit of insane rage rushed into a 'stockinger's' house [where people worked at stocking-frames, or early knitting machines], and destroyed two frames so completely that the saying 'Lud must have been here' came to be used throughout the hosiery districts when a stocking-frame had undergone extraordinary damage. The story lacks confirmation. It appears that in 1811 – 13 the nickname 'Captain Ludd' or 'King Lud' was commonly given to the ringleaders of the Luddites."

Other sources call Ludd a "mythical leader", or simply say, "There was no such person as Ludd." (Connolly, Sean. *The Industrial Revolution*. Oxford: Heinemann Library, 2003.)

This illustration shows British Luddite protesters rioting in 1813. It was drawn later in the 19th century by the English artist Hablot Knight Browne (1815–82), known as "Phiz".

Exploring books

You will most likely find a great deal of information about the Industrial Revolution in books available in your school and local lending and reference libraries. Since you can't (and do not want to) borrow too many books, you need to be able to decide quickly whether a particular book will be useful for your research. You may just want to take a few notes from a book while you're in the library, or even photocopy some pages. The book will probably include a description on the back cover or on the inside flap of a **dust jacket**. Remember that this description is written to promote the book, so it may simply praise the book's contents. There may be a more accurate description of the book in a preface, foreword, or introduction in which the author or another expert tells the reader the purpose of the book and its general subject matter. Some online bookshops, like Amazon, provide content notes on the books they sell which can be a useful way to find out what a book covers.

Is the content right?

The best way to get a quick overview of a book's subject matter is to look at the table of contents (sometimes called the contents list). The contents are listed at the beginning of a book and list chapter headings and their page numbers in the order in which they appear in the book. The list of contents serves as an outline. Some large reference books give further information under the chapter listings, such as subheads or other special features.

Indexes

If you are looking for a specific topic, such as "Industrial Revolution" in a history encyclopedia or "Luddites" in a book on 19th-century Britain, the place to look is the index. Most **non-fiction books** have an index, usually at the very end of the book.

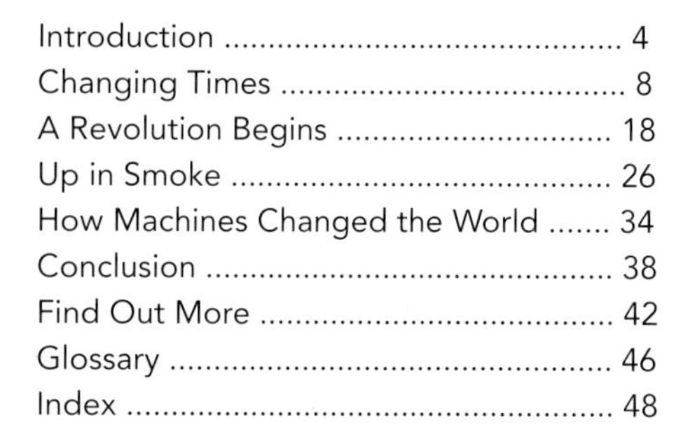

An index is a list of terms, subjects, names, and places in alphabetical order and with page numbers where the items can be found. Page references for illustrations are sometimes printed in italic or bold type. Some indexes may have sub-entries, indented under the main entry. For example, you might find a topic such as "working conditions" under "factories". An index will also be useful when you have looked through the book and want to review certain topics again.

Online index

Here is an example of what you can expect to find in an online index.

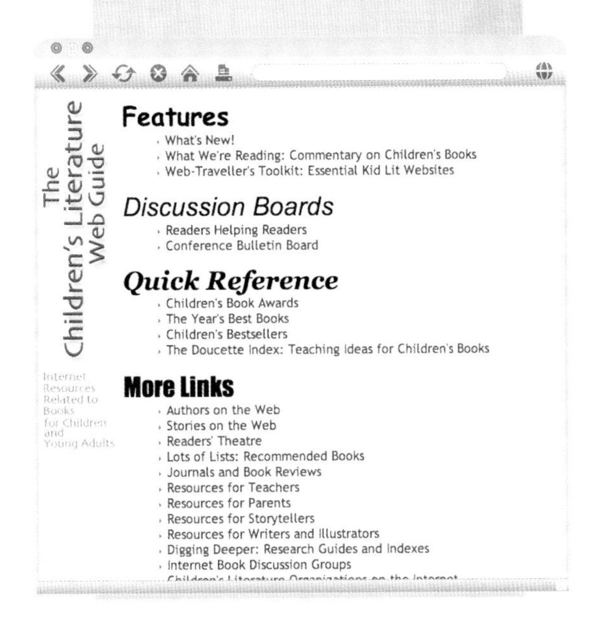

Encyclopedias

An encyclopedia is a large reference work that contains information on a wide range of subjects. Most encyclopedias are written by people who use special skills to ensure that the content is accurate. A general encyclopedia covers a wide range of important topics. There are also specialist encyclopedias, including some that cover history. The term encyclopedia comes from Greek words meaning "all-round education". In the past, these all-round books of knowledge were published as a set of large volumes. You can still find these in libraries.

Today you can also get entire encyclopedias on CD or DVD, at a fraction of the cost of the print editions. You may even find an encyclopedia software programme. Alternatively, you can subscribe to an encyclopedia online, or access one for free using your public library card. Remember that some encyclopedias are for a general, adult readership, while others are specifically aimed at students.

Searching the Internet

Searching the Internet is done using a **search engine**, such as Google or Yahoo! A search engine can be extremely helpful, but only if you use the search sensibly. Type "Industrial Revolution" into Google, and you will get millions of results. The exact number you will get changes all the time, as the search engines trawl the web constantly. With so many results, where do you begin?

The search engine lists each entry, followed by a couple of sentences containing the searched text and the **URL** of the webpage. Remember, all the search engine is doing is giving you a list of sites that contain your search words. Check out these websites, and you may well find links from them to other useful sites. But remember, the search engine is just the beginning of your research. It is a tool to get you started. It cannot complete your research by itself.

Wikipedia and others

One of the first search engine results might be an article in *Wikipedia*, which describes itself as "a multilingual, web-based, free-content encyclopedia project ... written collaboratively by volunteers from all around the world." The site has more than 75,000 contributors and attracts 684 million visitors every year. It is a huge, up-to-date resource – but can it be trusted? Most of its entries are probably as accurate as most other resources, but of course it is open to accidental mistakes and even intentional misuse. Since those mistakes could be in the particular article you are using, you must always back up any *Wikipedia* facts with other sources. You can often do this with the help of notes and other references that appear at the bottom of a *Wikipedia* article. These are the equivalent of footnotes in books, but have the advantage that you can click on them to quickly access the original source. You could also try sites like www.answers.com that give information from several sources, including *Wikipedia*.

Concept web

You can clarify your own thinking and organize the topics of your research by creating a **concept web** (see page 21). The key subject, topic, or research question comes at the centre of the web. Topics related to the key subject or involved in the answer to the question are added to boxes linked to the centre. Each of these topics (such as "Transport", "Factories", and "Replaced other forms of energy" in the concept web on page 21) will have further sub-topics or subheadings. These are supporting facts or details important in building your answer to the central question. Some of these facts may come from your KWL chart (see page 16). You can include facts you already knew before (from the first column), as well as those you have learned during the research process.

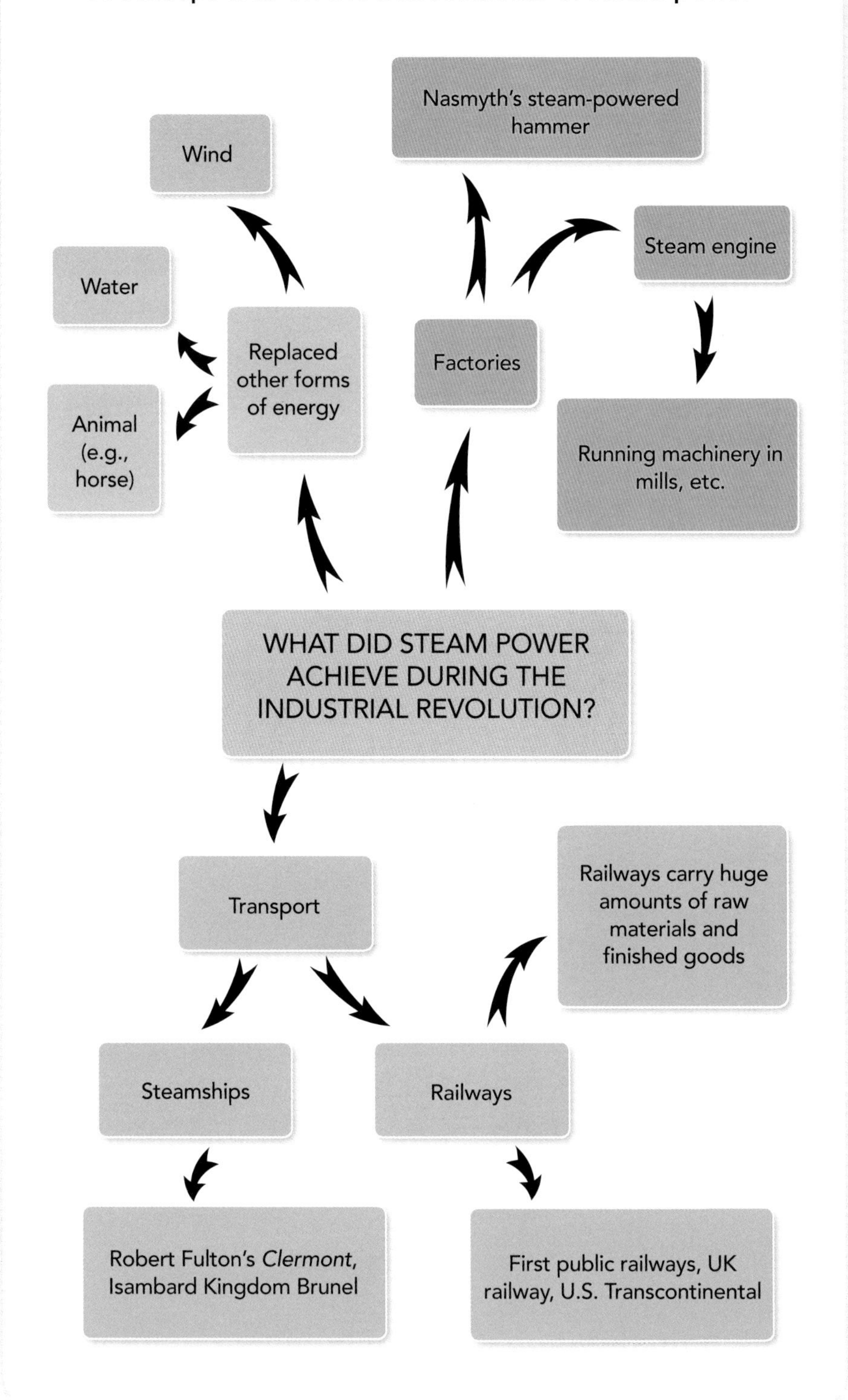
A concept web on the achievements of steam power
Nasmyth's steam-powered hammer
Wind
Steam engine
Water
Replaced other forms of energy
Factories
Animal (e.g., horse)
Running machinery in mills, etc.
WHAT DID STEAM POWER ACHIEVE DURING THE INDUSTRIAL REVOLUTION?
Transport
Railways carry huge amounts of raw materials and finished goods
Steamships
Railways
Robert Fulton's Clermont, Isambard Kingdom Brunel
First public railways, UK railway, U.S. Transcontinental

Narrowing a Topic

When researching a broad subject such as the Industrial Revolution, you will want to make things more manageable by reducing the subject to more specific topics. There are several ways to do this. You could type the subject into the online catalogue of your library, which will display related topics. Another good place to look would be the table of contents or index of relevant books on the subject. An Internet search engine will also help you to find topics related to a broad subject.

Related topics

One related topic to our overall subject is factories. You may find a chapter on this topic in a book about the Industrial Revolution that will tell you the factory system developed because merchants wanted to find ways of producing goods more efficiently and economically. They wanted to develop ways of getting their workers to produce more goods in less time. This became possible by placing powered machines all in one place – a factory.

Types of factories

You might then narrow your topic further to investigate specific types of factories. For example, one of the most important kinds of factories was the textile mill, where wool and cotton were spun and woven into fabric. At first water power was used to drive textile machines, and this was later replaced by steam.

Working conditions

As you continue to research textile mills, you may come across information on factory conditions. For example, a typical mill in Lancashire, in the north of England, employed fewer than 100 workers. They worked long hours and kept the machines running day and night by working in shifts. Many of the workers were children, some as young as five years old. The factory owners paid children less than they would have to pay adults.

In 1833 the first effective laws against child labour were passed. They made it illegal for children under the age of nine years old to work, older children were not permitted to work at night, and the working day for under-18s was cut to 12 hours.

Creating a triangle chart

Thinking of a triangle may help you to see how you can narrow your subject. You could create a graphic organizer by drawing a triangle that points downwards. Using the topics or terms that you find in your research, fill in the narrowing triangle, starting from the top. This clearly shows how you are narrowing the subject, and you can finish with a topic that might be used to answer a particular question or solve a problem.

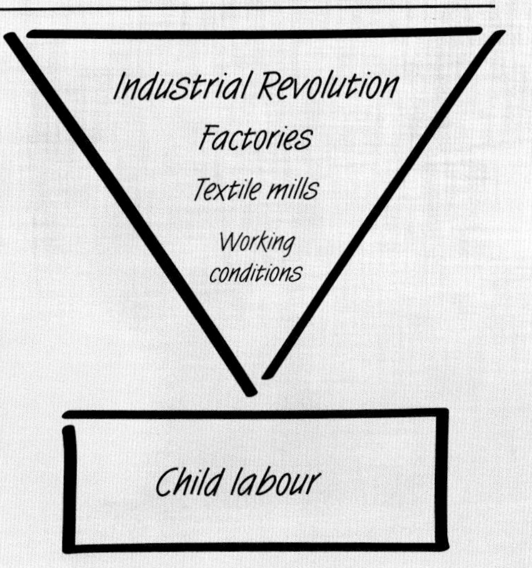

Speeding things up

Another important step in narrowing a subject is quickly locating information that is useful to you. When you find a relevant book or website, you do not necessarily want to read the whole thing. You simply want to take out of each resource what you need. There are two important techniques that can help you: **skimming** and **scanning**.

Skimming

Skimming can help you to determine quickly if the text that you have found contains useful information about your topic. You can then decide whether it is worth reading the text in more detail. Skimming is used to get the overall sense of a piece of text.

When you skim, you don't read all the text word for word. Instead, you let your eyes skim over the text and look out for important, useful points. Here are the steps to follow:

- Read the title and any subtitle.
- Quickly look through the first paragraph or introduction.
- Read all headings and subheadings.
- Read the first and last sentence of each paragraph.
- Look at any illustrations (photographs, drawings, diagrams, and charts) and glance at their **captions**.
- Look out for **key words** and read those that are in bold type or italics.
- Look through the last paragraph and any summary or conclusion.

Scanning

Another fast-reading technique is called scanning. You can use it to locate specific information in a piece of text, especially information that can help you answer a research question. When you scan, you don't need to read or understand every word. You simply check the page for key words – such as names, dates, and locations – or important phrases. The difference between scanning and skimming is that when you scan, you are looking for something specific. Here are some tips for successful scanning:

- Focus your mind by telling yourself exactly what you are looking for. It might help to put this in the form of a question.
- Think about how the answer will appear and what clues you can use to find it.
- Don't try to read every word, but scan through text and let your eyes move quickly down the page.
- Use headings, subheadings, and bold and italic type to identify sections where the information you need might be found.

Navigating websites

If you use the Internet to narrow down a broad subject, you will have to navigate (or find your way around) many different kinds of websites. They may have separate sections (or groups of pages) to which you can jump by clicking on a separate tab or button. For example, the Science Museum's web page on Stephenson's *Rocket* Locomotive of 1829 (www.sciencemuseum.org.uk/objects/nrm_-_locomotives_and_rolling_stock/1862-5.aspx) has a series of buttons across the top of the page, including

- Home
- Visit the museum
- About us

The home page is the starting point for all websites. Simply click on the "Home" button to start again. The "About us" section is often very useful, because it gives you the source of the website so that you can judge how much you can rely on the information it contains.

Some websites have contents lists similar to those you find in books. They may also have hyperlinks which appear in blue and become underlined when you place your cursor on them. You can then click to go straight to that information.

Some website entries contain lists of other related articles. For example, in the article for "Industrial Revolution", you can scan the contents and click on "Railways" under "Transport in Britain".

If you scan this article, you will see that there is a hyperlink to another *Wikipedia* article called "History of rail transport in Great Britain".

This is an engraving (a kind of artist's print) of George Stephenson's locomotive Rocket (seen at the front) at the 1829 Rainhill trials of early steam locomotives. This competition, held near Liverpool, was organized to select the best design of steam engine for the new Liverpool to Manchester railway. It is a good image to use to illustrate text on early steam trains.

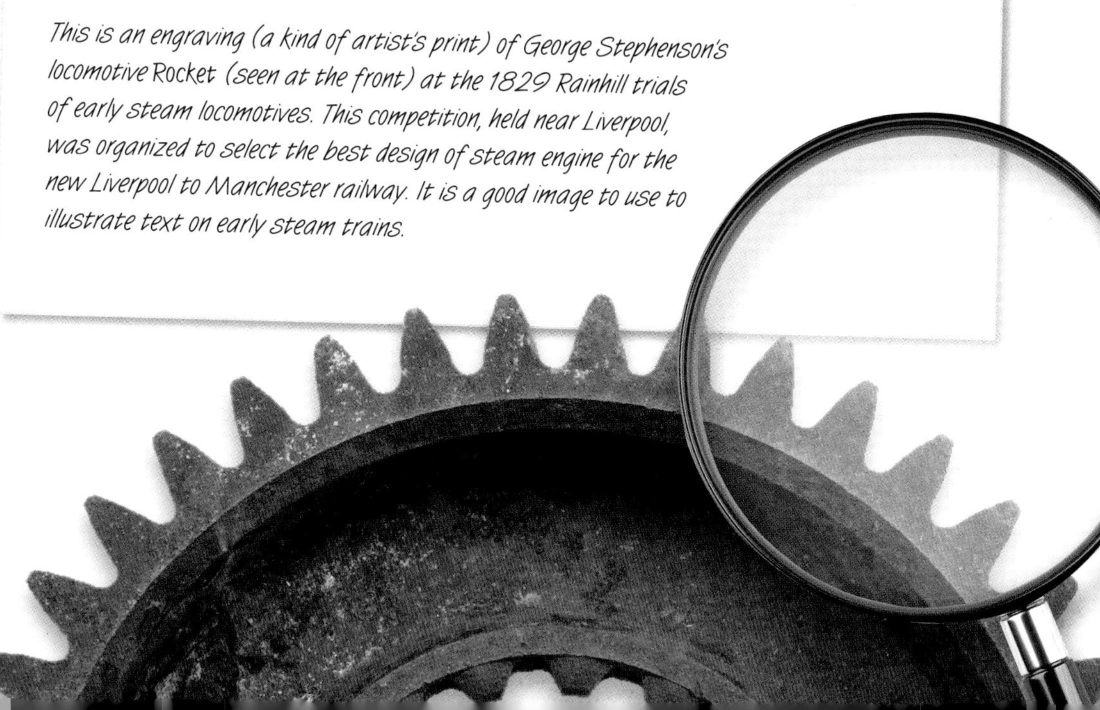

Checking Sources

As noted on page 5, secondary sources are made up of works written at a later time about the period in question. In other words, secondary sources are the results of other people's research. For example, the results of your research will be a secondary source. In your own work, you will come across many different sources. Some will be more useful than others, and you will need to be able to compare and evaluate all these sources. When you evaluate them, you judge their importance, value, reliability, and quality. One way to do this is to use the 5 Ws technique.

The 5 Ws

The idea of this technique is that you can evaluate information by asking five basic questions: **W**ho, **W**hat, **W**here, **W**hen, and **W**hy? The answers to these questions will help you to determine the accuracy and relevance of information. Questions you could ask about each 5 W when researching a history topic include:

Who?

- Who is the author of the text?
- Is the author an expert on the subject (e.g., a historian)?
- Is a biography of the author included so you can learn more about her or him?

What?

- What is the purpose of the text?
- What else might the author have in mind for this text?

Where?

- Where did the information come from?
- Is the information **biased** in any way?
- Does the information appear to be accurate?

When?

- When was the text written?
- Is the information as up to date as it needs to be (depending on your research question)?

Why?

- Why is this information useful to you?
- Why is this source useful, and is it better than others?

5 Ws and an H

In 1902, Rudyard Kipling included a poem in his story called "The Elephant's Child". The poem begins:

> "I keep six honest serving-men
> (They taught me all I knew);
> Their names are What and Why and When
> And How and Where and Who."

The question "How?" is often added to the 5 Ws list by journalists and researchers. You could ask, "How is this information useful?"

Citations

It is important to organize your sources as you take notes on your subject, and you must keep track of them all. As you do your research, you should write down all the sources you think might be useful later. One of the easiest ways to do this is to use index cards (see page 34). Keeping your sources organized means that you can **cite** them. How you do this will depend on the requirements of your project. If you are not sure what is required in terms of citations, discuss this with your teacher.

Bookmarking online sources

If you are working on your own computer, you can keep a note of Internet sources by using your browser's "Bookmarks" list (sometimes called "Favorites"). When you find a useful web page, go to the browser's "Bookmarks" menu and add the page to the list. The URL (web address) is then saved, and you can retrieve it at any time. You can organize all your bookmarks into separate folders, so you could have one for factories, another for steam power, and so on. They could then all go into a main folder called "The Industrial Revolution".

Bibliography

A **bibliography** (from the ancient Greek word for "writing books") is an organized list of books and other sources. It normally appears in alphabetical order at the end of a report. The list should include all the sources that you have used for writing your report, and possibly some you have only referred to. As a general rule, each entry in a bibliography will include the author, title, publisher, and date of publication. Sometimes the place of publication is given, too.

Bibliography entries

There are many ways to create a bibliography. Talk to your teacher about what method is required, and then use the same method for all your sources. Here are just a few examples:

Book
Author's last name, first name. Title of Book. Place of publication: publisher, date of publication.

Example: Connolly, Sean. *The Industrial Revolution*. Oxford: Heinemann Library, 2003.

Magazine/journal/periodical
Author's last name, first name. "Title of article." Title of Magazine/ Newspaper. Volume, date: page number(s).

Example: Mockler, R.A. "Coming of the Railways." *Historical Review*. No. 45, 2007: 44–46.

Encyclopedia
(If known) Article author's last name, first name. "Title of article." Title of encyclopedia. Volume, date of publication.

Example: "Industrial Revolution." *Encyclopaedia Britannica*, Online Library Edition. 17, 2008.

Website
(If known) Author's last name, first name. "Title of article." Title of webpage. Copyright date or revision date. Publisher of web page. Day month year you saw the site. Web address

Example: "Inventions." Edison Birthplace Museum. 1997-2009. Edison Birthplace Association, Inc. 27 Jan 2009. www.tomedison.org/invent.html

Footnotes and endnotes

Depending on instructions from your teacher, you may need to cite the sources you use at particular points in your report. You can do this by including a small number (like this[1]) at the appropriate point in the text. Alternatively, an asterisk (*) or dagger (†) can be used to mark text. The number or mark draws attention to a footnote at the bottom of the page (or sometimes at the end of a section or chapter). The footnote may list a full source, in the same way and in a similar style as in a bibliography. It may just contain a short reference to a source that is fully described in the bibliography.

Endnotes work in exactly the same way as footnotes, except that they appear at the end rather than throughout the work. If you are using a word processing program, such as Microsoft Word, to write your report, it can help you create footnotes or endnotes. You can automatically add number marks, and when you add, delete, or move notes that are automatically numbered, the program will renumber them so that they are still in sequence.

A sample bibliography (book list)

Connolly, Sean. *The Industrial Revolution.* Oxford: Heinemann Library, 2003.

Deane, Phyllis. *The First Industrial Revolution.* Cambridge: Cambridge University Press, 1980.

King, Catherine. *Women of Iron.* London: Sphere, 2007.

Pinchbeck, Ivy. *Women Workers and the Industrial Revolution, 1750–1850.* London: Virago, 1981.

Ross, Stewart. *History in Writing: The Industrial Revolution.* London: Evans, 1999.

Smith, Nigel. *Events and Outcomes: The Industrial Revolution.* London: Evans, 2002.

Tames, Richard. *Turning Points: The Steam Engine.* Oxford: Heinemann Library, 1999.

Reading lists

A reading list is quite different from a bibliography. It is a list of books that are recommended by an expert (or perhaps by your teacher) as being useful sources of information. A reading list may include both primary and secondary sources.

How many sources?

Your teacher may give you specific instructions about the number and type of sources you need to use. If not, you will have to decide for yourself how many you need. Your decisions will depend on the kind of information and the reliability of each particular source. Some facts are considered common knowledge, and these can be confirmed by one reliable source. An example would be the dates of famous events, such as the year that Queen Victoria came to the throne in Britain (1837), or the year when the transcontinental railway was completed across the United States (1869).

Even if you are sure you know the date or another fact, you should check it in a reliable source. Otherwise, it is easy to make mistakes. If a fact is less clear or open to debate, you should confirm it in at least two reliable sources. Sometimes you simply may not be able to verify a fact in a second source. You may be confident that it is true, in which case you could use a phrase such as, "Although it is unconfirmed, *Industrial Digest* magazine claims that ...".

When sources disagree

When you try to confirm a fact, you may occasionally find that sources disagree. You might be happy to trust the most reliable source, or you could mention the disagreement in your report (by saying "Some sources suggest ...", for example). Some facts, such as population figures, may be listed differently in equally reliable sources. This is especially the case with websites, which are constantly updated. The authors of books and encyclopedias may have different ways of gathering information and may use different sources themselves.

For example, *The London Encyclopaedia* (published in a revised edition by Macmillan in 1995) gives historical population figures for London as:

1801	959,301
1851	2,363,341
1891	4,227,954

This is a very reliable reference work, but other sources might give slightly different figures. You could get around this by writing something like: "The population of London grew from fewer than a million in 1801 to more than 2 million by the middle of the century. By 1891 there were more than 4 million people in London."

Using the SQ3R technique

SQ3R stands for **S**urvey, **Q**uestion, **R**ead, **R**ecite, and **R**eview. This technique can help you to organize your research.

Survey ...

- a work's title, chapter, and spread headings and subheadings, as well as captions to pictures, charts, graphs, and maps
- the introduction and conclusion or summary, for major ideas
- review questions and educational study guides.

Question

- Turn the title, headings, and subheadings into questions.
- What question is this work (or section) trying to answer?
- Read any questions that appear at the end of sections or chapters.
- Ask yourself, "What did my teacher say about this subject or chapter when the project was assigned?"
- Ask yourself, "What do I already know about this subject?"

Read

- Look for answers to the questions that appear at the end of chapters or in an educational study guide.
- Reread captions to pictures, charts, graphs, and maps.
- Note all words or phrases that are underlined, italic, or bold.
- Read difficult passages more slowly.
- Stop and reread any passages that are not clear.
- Read a section at a time.

Recite

- Say questions out loud about what you have just read.
- Take notes from the text, but **summarize** information in your own words.
- If using photocopies, underline or highlight important points.
- Recite answers out loud, remembering that the more sensible your answers, the more likely you are to remember what you read.

Review ...

- the key phrases and other notes you made within 24 hours of making the notes
- again after one week
- about once a month until the time of your presentation (or exam).

Primary Source Material

Primary sources mainly consist of written documents from the time, such as books, diaries, and letters, created by the people involved. Newspapers and official documents from the time can also be interesting and helpful. Many primary source documents relating to the Industrial Revolution are kept in **archives** in libraries or museums. In your research, you may not come across much original material. Nevertheless, it is important to look at photographs or copies of primary sources, especially to get a real feel for the period that you are researching.

Secondary checking

You will find many primary sources reprinted in books and websites that you consult as secondary sources. In fact, this is a good way to find primary sources. Most books that quote original material will list their sources on the relevant page or at the end of the book. You can then check this source, either by finding the book in a library or, if an Internet source is given, by looking at the quoted web page. See the example on page 33 of a search for an original description of the first successful steamboat voyage.

*This **re-enactment** of the first voyage of the steamboat Clermont took place in the United States around 1930. It presents an interesting image of what the original event in 1807 may have looked like.*

The first successful steamboat voyage: Author Neil Morris's research journey

Looking through a history book about the Industrial Revolution, I found a supposedly original letter from Robert Fulton to his friend Joel Barlow, dated 17 August 1807. Fulton was the American engineer who built the first successful steamboat in 1807. In the book, the letter was handwritten, but obviously by a modern writer. I wondered if the transcription was correct. A list of primary sources at the end of the book quoted a website source from the University of Rochester, New York, but it turned out that this page no longer existed. However, a look at the university's home page brought up a page called "Steam engine library", and listed on this was a book called *Robert Fulton: His Life and Its Results*, by Robert H. Thurston (Dodd, Mead, and Company Publishers, New York, 1891).

By using the computer "Find" facility and typing in the first words of the quote I wanted, I found the passage. Then, by putting the same words into Google, I found another old book – *History of American Steam Navigation* by John Harrison Morrison, originally published in 1903 (reprinted by Read Books, 2008) – with the same text. Apart from some slight differences in spelling, they were exactly the same and published very soon after the actual event. This was the sort of primary source that I was after, and I could now be confident that it was reliable. Incidentally, it turned out that the text in the original book from which I started from was also correct.

Here is the text from the beginning of Robert Fulton's letter:

"My steamboat voyage to Albany and back has turned out rather more favorably than I had calculated. The distance from New York to Albany is one hundred and fifty miles. I ran it up in thirty-two hours, and down in thirty. I had a light breeze against me the whole way, both going and coming, and the voyage has been performed wholly by the power of the steam-engine. I overtook many sloops and schooners beating to windward, and parted with them as if they had been at anchor. The power of propelling boats by steam is now fully proved."

National archives

- In the UK, the National Archives offer the DocumentsOnline service (see www.nationalarchives.gov.uk/documentsonline/). This allows you access to the National Archives' collection of digitized public records by using a search button.

Keeping notes

A good way to keep track of all your sources is to write them down on index cards (sometimes called notecards). Card index systems were common before the days of personal computers, and they are still very useful. You can write and keep a separate card for every useful source you find, and you can add notes on the importance of the source, as well as quotations. Don't forget to write down the page number if the source comes from a book. You can speed things up by using abbreviations for book titles. Index cards like the examples below can be used later when you compile your bibliography.

Definition of Ind. Rev.:
EB [abbreviation for Encyclopaedia Britannica], in article "History of Technology" section Industrial Revolution (1750-1900)

Industrial Revolution describes period of time but is not precise. Has no clear beginning or end. Phrase is used to describe faster rate of growth and change, or first 150 years of this period of time.

Fact: occurred first in Britain, gradually spread to Europe and North America

Railways, building:
FWTE [From Workshop to Empire], p 50.

Useful (horrific!) quote. Newspaper report, Liverpool Mercury, 10 August 1827.

"We are pained to state that a labourer, who was working in the excavation of the rail-road, at Edgehill, ... was killed on Monday last. The poor fellow was in the act of undermining a heavy head of clay, 14 or 15 feet high, when the mass fell upon him, and literally crushed his bowels out of his body."

Social commentary

During the Industrial Revolution in many parts of the world, social commentators, critics, novelists, and poets gave their opinions on how society was changing. Many of the opinions were critical. Such voices, especially famous ones, can be interesting and add to the fund of primary sources. In Britain, two of the most famous critics of aspects of the Industrial Revolution were Thomas Carlyle (1795–1881) and John Ruskin (1819–1900).

Scottish historian and essayist Carlyle wrote about the social problems and divisions between working-class poverty and middle-class wealth. In *Past and Present* (1843), Carlyle criticized social conditions caused by industrial development. Ruskin wrote about social issues, too, questioning the capitalist system of free enterprise and criticizing the lack of quality of mass-produced goods.

Literature

Novels can also tell us something about a period's social conditions. One of the greatest writers on English society was Charles Dickens (1812–70) (see page 37). In France, Émile Zola (1840–1902) wrote novels about working-class life in industrial regions. His masterpiece *Germinal* (1885) shows the hardships of a mining community. The novel recounts the events of a miners' strike, comparing the coalmine to an all-devouring monster.

Poets also wrote about the effects of the Industrial Revolution. A famous example is Elizabeth Barrett Browning (1806–61), who wrote *The Cry of the Children* in 1843. In this poem, she tells of the terrible effects of child labour in 19th-century factories and mines:

> Let them feel that this cold metallic motion
> Is not all the life God fashions or reveals:
> Let them prove their living souls against the notion
> That they live in you, or under you, O wheels!
> Still, all day, the iron wheels go onward,
> Grinding life down from its mark.

Writers often bring the power of their own imaginations to their work. This means that their descriptions of events and conditions may be biased and not strictly accurate. But they help to paint a picture of the background to a period or location.

Online books

Because they are out of copyright, many 19th-century novels, poems, and other works are available in full online. Enter a work's title and author into a search engine to see if it is available. Of course, most are also available in print in libraries.

Industrial sources

Many trade unions and other industrial groups kept records and journals. These can tell us a great deal about life for ordinary workers. A good example is the *Lowell Offering*, a monthly **periodical** published between 1840 and 1845 in Lowell, Massachusetts. This journal contained poems, stories, and other writings by female textile mill workers. You can read the works by visiting the website of the University of Massachusetts Center for Lowell History (http://library.uml.edu/clh/Offering.htm).

These young "breaker boys" had the tough job of separating coal from slate and other rocks. The photograph was taken at a mine in the U.S. state of Pennsylvania in 1891.

Using images

Images such as paintings and engravings can be useful both for understanding the period and for presenting in your report. Photographs are also instructive and helpful, but of course there was very little photography before the middle of the 19th century. Until the early 20th century, many photographers deliberately dramatized events and situations in their work, rather than simply recording events. This can be true of all artists and illustrators, which means that you should treat images with great caution. Do they show a real situation, such as working conditions in a factory, or has the scene been set up? It is very difficult to find the answers to questions like these, but it is always important to ask questions about the source.

Check out the book, journal, or website where you found the image. Then read the caption or accompanying text carefully. Ask yourself what exactly it is that you are seeing? Commercial picture library sites can be helpful, but very often their captions are brief and uninformative. Also, you cannot reproduce their images without permission.

Charles Dickens

Through his novels, Dickens was known as a champion of the poor and helpless, and a fierce critic of the abuse of wealth and power. Two of his novels are particularly suited to a study of conditions in industrial Britain. *Oliver Twist* (published as a monthly serial from 1837–39) describes the adventures of a poor orphan boy in a workhouse. *Hard Times* (a weekly serial from 1854) is set in a fictitious industrial town in northern England. The background to the novel is Dickens' criticism of a Utilitarian philosophy based on a belief that human actions and institutions should be judged by their usefulness. Dickens believed this rational approach led to too much self interest in powerful people and led to misery for the working class. A factory owner, for example, could think that it was right to pay workers poorly so that he made more money and could expand or build more factories.

Dickens also wrote a book about conditions in the United States. *American Notes for General Circulation* (1842) describes a trip Dickens took to North America. In the book he describes what he likes and dislikes about the American way of life. Just as his hatred of poverty comes through in his novels, here he aims his greatest criticism at slavery, which then still flourished in the southern states. Dickens also visited factories, such as those in Lowell, Massachusetts. He was favourably impressed by the working conditions of the young women in the textile mills.

Further Evidence

Historians and professional researchers look into specialist sources to learn more about their particular subject. Depending on where you live, you could visit places that will tell you a lot more about the Industrial Revolution. You could ask your teacher about local and regional museums, which might even have special visiting days for students and school groups.

Cotton topic

Visits to specialist museums can be useful when you are researching a specific topic. A good example is the topic of cotton, which was exported from the United States across the Atlantic Ocean during the Industrial Revolution, linking Britain and the USA. Both countries have many cotton and textile museums that can be visited today.

During the 18th century, British **entrepreneurs** tried to keep their new technological advances to themselves, because they didn't want other people competing with their businesses. As cotton growing expanded on

This illustration appeared in the American magazine Harper's Weekly *in the 1860s. It shows black slaves operating a cotton gin, while landowners discuss the machine.*

the other side of the Atlantic, American colonists exported the raw material to England, where it was spun and woven into textiles. In 1793, Eli Whitney (1765–1825) developed a machine called a cotton gin, which separated the cotton plant's seeds from its fibres quickly and efficiently.

One gin could do the work of 50 people in the same time. This led to cotton mills being built in New England and the expansion of the cotton-picking industry in the southern states. This in turn led to growth in the American slave population in the early 19th century, as southern plantation owners and farmers needed more workers to pick cotton. Here is a sub-topic that would be well worth exploring further: How did the development of the cotton industry promote slavery and become a cause of the American Civil War?

Mills and museums

There are several restored cotton mills in the north of England. One of the earliest is Sir Richard Arkwright's Masson Mills in Matlock Bath, Derbyshire, which was built in 1783. The building now contains a working textile museum (see www.massonmills.co.uk). At the Textile Museum in Helmshore, Lancashire, you can visit the restored buildings of Higher Mill (built in 1789) and Whitaker's Mill (1857). Visitors can explore the different machinery used to turn raw cotton into spun yarn ready for weaving (for more information, see www.lancashire.gov.uk/acs/sites/museums/venues/helmshore/index.asp.)

Letter from Thomas Jefferson

While researching this piece on cotton, the author of this book came across a reference to a letter written on 16 November 1793 to Eli Whitney by Thomas Jefferson (1743–1826), the U.S. secretary of state who later became president. He found a copy of the letter on an academic website. (see http://www.library.yale.edu/mssa/elms/images/0003.gif). Part of the text of the letter reads:

"As the state of Virginia, of which I am, carries on household manufactures of cotton to a great extent, as I also do myself, and one of our great embarrassments is the clearing the cotton of the seed, I feel a considerable interest in the success of your invention, for family use."

These female workers in a Manchester cotton mill were photographed around 1909. Some cotton mills and their original machinery are preserved as museums, including Quarry Bank in Cheshire. See http://www.nationaltrust.org.uk/main/w-quarrybankmillandstyalestate for more information.

Local history

You will be able to use your research skills to find out more about your local area. You could investigate local history during the relevant period and compare this with national developments of the Industrial Revolution. Were developments similar where you live to those in the rest of the country?

Hands-on research

Many science museums have interactive exhibits, from which students can learn a great deal. Some museums have originals while others have replicas of revolutionary industrial inventions. A good example is the Science Museum in London (see www.sciencemuseum.org.uk/), where displays in the Energy Hall include the oldest surviving atmospheric engine built by Francis

Thompson, rotative engines built by James Watt, high-pressure steam engines pioneered by Richard Trevithick, and a steam turbine designed by Charles Parsons. There is also a mill engine that drove 1,700 power looms for weaving textiles in Burnley, Lancashire. Even Stephenson's *Rocket* locomotive is there.

Ironbridge

The famous first cast-iron bridge, in Shropshire, was a marvel of industrial architecture. Its iron arches were each cast in two halves, using a total of nearly 400 tonnes of cast iron. Though closed to traffic, the bridge still stands at its original spot today.

Ironbridge Gorge, on the River Severn in the West Midlands region of England, was named after its most famous landmark – the world's first cast-iron bridge. This was a hugely important event in the history of the Industrial Revolution in Britain, where it all began. It showed that iron could be used for large, complex designs, which was useful because of the material's strength. The bridge was built in 1779 by Abraham Darby III, grandson of the iron manufacturer who built the first coke-fired blast furnace 70 years earlier at nearby Coalbrookdale. In the late 18th century, many furnaces, factories, and workshops along this stretch of the Severn made it one of Europe's busiest rivers.

The iron bridge on the River Severn was repaired and renovated many times, and remained open to vehicles for 155 years. The first iron bridge still stands today, spanning 30 metres (100 feet) across the river. Several museums are located near the famous bridge and the old ironworks. One is Coalbrookdale Museum of Iron, where visitors can see the remains of Darby's blast furnace. Visit www.ironbridge.org.uk to find out more about the Ironbridge Gorge.

Forming an Opinion

In order to be able to form an opinion on an issue, you have to evaluate information. During your research on the Industrial Revolution, you will come across a huge amount of information. You will need to weigh up the evidence presented in the sources in order to decide whether the facts given are correct and therefore helpful to you.

You must also decide whether pieces of information are facts or opinions. Sometimes it is clear from the way in which the information is conveyed that it is an opinion, or that it is a widely held belief that can be considered almost a fact. Compare these three sentences about James Watt. The first two are from *World Book Encyclopedia's* article on Watt. The third is written by the author of this book:

- In 1757, Watt became instrument maker at the University of Glasgow.
- Watt's later improvements made possible the wide application of steam engines, contributing much to the growth of modern industry.
- Watt was the most important inventor of the Industrial Revolution.

This undated hand-coloured engraving shows James Watt working on improvements to a model steam engine developed by Thomas Newcomen. Watt did this work around 1763.

The first is a statement of fact, which you can verify in other sources. *Encylopedia Britannica*, for example, says: "Returning to Glasgow, [Watts] opened a shop in 1757 at the university and made mathematical instruments (e.g., quadrants, compasses, scales)." The second statement is a combination of fact and informed opinion. You will quickly gather from reading other sources about James Watt that it would be difficult to disagree with or argue against this statement. The third sentence is very different, and is an opinion. You would also gather from other sources that this is not a widely held opinion, and most writers would not make such a statement, which is anyway fairly meaningless (What does "most important" mean?).

A-R-E

When you want to state your opinion or put forward your point of view, you can use the **A-R-E** approach. The letters stand for **A**ssertion-**R**easoning-**E**vidence. First you make an assertion, which is a statement that something is true. Then you back this up with reasoning, which is the use of logical thinking. Finally, you present evidence based on facts for the point of view.

Is this person really important?

As you will see from the timeline on pages 12–15, many individuals contributed to the Industrial Revolution. The entry on Isambard Kingdom Brunel (1806–59) is a general one, because he achieved so much in his life, which covered the first half of the 19th century. Here is a list of some of the structures and ships he created:

Date	Event
1825–28	Thames Tunnel, London
1833–59	Tracks, bridges, tunnels, and stations of the Great Western Railway
1837	*Great Western*, the earliest regular transatlantic steamship
1843	*Great Britain*, the first propeller-driven iron steamship
1858	*Great Eastern*, then the largest ship ever built, with two paddle engines, two screw engines, and sails rigged on six masts
1864	Clifton Suspension Bridge over River Avon in Bristol (completed after Brunel's death)
1859	Royal Albert Bridge over the River Tamar on the Devon–Cornwall border

Not everyone makes an interesting biographical subject, but by reading the facts of a person's life, you can form your own opinion about his or her importance.

Bias and propaganda

Researchers must always be on the lookout for bias in the various primary and secondary sources they consult, including unregulated online sites. One of the ways to detect a prejudiced approach is to ask yourself questions such as: Why is the information here, and what is its purpose? If, for example, you were reading accounts of an important event in a nation's history by reporters from that same country, you might expect them to be favourable. You might even find that they are over-enthusiastic, and that might lead you to think that they are biased and unreliable as factual reports.

Taking a line

You may wish or be required to express your own opinions on issues raised by your research. These may include social or political issues, on which there are opposing points of view and it is difficult to make a judgement. If you do decide to take sides, you should make it clear that you are doing so and give sources for your opinion. If you are undecided, you might wish to present evidence for both sides of the argument.

Writing techniques

During your research you will come across texts written in many different styles. In the case of the Industrial Revolution, the sources you consult will be mainly informative, presenting facts in a straightforward way. When you are reading any text, you should always think about its purpose and why it has been written. This will help you detect bias.

Types of writing

	Aim	Examples
Informative	Gives information based on facts.	Research report
Narrative	Tells a story, describing people, places, and events.	Novel, short story, letter
Persuasive	Aims to convince the reader of a point of view.	Sales brochure, advertisement
Instructive	Tells you how to do something.	Computer manual, car handbook

The Great Exhibition: National and international propaganda

The Great Exhibition was held in London in 1851. It displayed more than 100,000 industrial exhibits from all over the world, but most were British. This was an opportunity to show Britain off as the "workshop of the world" and to win new orders both at home and abroad. The exhibition was a huge success. It ran for 20 weeks and had more than 6 million visitors. It was opened by Queen Victoria, who wrote in her diary: "The tremendous cheers, the joy on every face, and all due to my husband [Prince Albert], the author of this 'Peace Festival' which united the industry and art of all nations." The queen enjoyed herself so much that she went to the exhibition over 40 times, visiting all the exhibits.

Much of the reporting of the Great Exhibition was so biased that you could almost call it propaganda (in other words, information used to promote the event rather than describe or review it). *The Illustrated London News* was positive in its reporting. Describing the exhibits in the Canadian Court, a journalist wrote that they showed "the industrial beginnings of a junior branch of the great civilizing family of the universe." The reporter was referring to the British Empire, of which the Victorians were extremely proud.

This print shows the crowds of visitors inside the Crystal Palace on the last day of the Great Exhibition, 15 October 1851. The Palace was put up in London's Hyde Park, and some trees were left standing inside the iron and glass structure.

Political viewpoint

In 1845 a book called *The Condition of the Working Class in England* by Frederick Engels was published. The author dedicated the book to working people and addressed them in his preface:

"Having … ample opportunity to watch the middle classes, your opponents, I soon came to the conclusion that you are right, perfectly right in expecting no support whatever from them. Their interest is diametrically opposed [opposite] to yours, though they always will try to maintain the contrary … the middle classes intend in reality nothing else but to enrich themselves by your labour while they can sell its produce, and to abandon you to starvation as soon as they cannot make a profit by this indirect trade in human flesh."

The book was very influential and is still in print today. In it, Engels argues that the Industrial Revolution was damaging to workers, leaving them exploited and ruining their health. His figures show that death rates amongst workers in British cities such as Manchester and Liverpool were much worse

This photograph from 1889 illustrates living conditions for the urban poor in the north-east of England at the time. The conditions of the working classes in England inspired the political philosophy of Frederick Engels and Karl Marx.

than in the countryside and much higher than the national average. The book was, and still is very convincing, but if we are using it as a source of information about the Industrial Revolution, we should perhaps take the author's political views into account.

Who was Frederick Engels?

Frederick Engels (1820–95) was a social scientist, philosopher, and journalist who became a political revolutionary. The son of a German textile manufacturer, he went to Manchester in 1842 to work for a textile firm in which his father was a shareholder. Five years later, he became a founder member, along with Karl Marx (1818–83), of the Communist League

In 1848 Marx and Engels published the *Communist Manifesto*. It doesn't necessarily follow that *The Condition of the Working Class in England* is communist propaganda. However, it is reasonable to assume that it is written from a particular viewpoint, which any researcher should consider when evaluating it.

Workhouse welfare?

The topic of workhouses is important in any study of the Industrial Revolution in Britain. The *Oxford English Dictionary* defines a workhouse as "A house established for the provision of work for the unemployed poor of a parish; later, an institution, administered by Guardians of the Poor, in which paupers were lodged and the able-bodied set to work." They sound like reasonable institutions, but did they really help people?

The National Trust owns a well-preserved workhouse at Southwell, in Nottinghamshire. On its website, the National Trust invites visitors to "explore the workshops and dormitories of this imposing early 'welfare' institution". The writer used the quotation marks around the word welfare in order to imply that the institution gave a different definition to welfare than what we understand today. Certainly conditions in workhouses were harsh. Men and women were segregated and children were taken away from their parents. Inmates had to wear a workhouse uniform, and food was dull and not very nutritious.

Presentation

The way in which you organize your research material will depend on how you intend to present your findings. Sometimes your teacher will tell you what sort of presentation is required. Other times you may need to choose for yourself.

The most common form of presentation is a written report. Before you start putting a report together, you must work out how to organize your findings into a coherent whole. This means planning your writing and thinking the whole report through at the beginning. The best way to do this is to create an outline, breaking your research findings down into sections or chapters.

How good is your writing?

It should be:

- clear and easy to read
- free of spelling and punctuation mistakes
- written in an appropriate form and style
- well organized and logical.

Paraphrasing and summarizing

Whatever kind of report you are producing, it is vitally important that you put all the information in your own words. The only exception to this is direct quotations, which you will cite in footnotes or endnotes. Any direct quotations should be identical to the original and must begin and end with quotation marks, to show that they are not your words.

- **Paraphrasing** means restating information from source material in your own words, and it usually involves making another piece of text, or several texts, shorter and simpler. If you decide to paraphrase a single source and keep the sense similar, you should mention or list the original source.
- **Summarizing** means giving a shortened version of a set of ideas or a piece of information. As you write your report, you might find that you can summarize your own findings and make a point in one sentence instead of a whole paragraph.

Plagiarism

If you were to take and use someone else's work, text, or ideas and pretend they were your own, you would be committing an act of **plagiarism**. The practice of plagiarism is cheating by copying, and obviously must be avoided at all costs. Copying is a very serious offence, which is one of the reasons why it is so important to log, keep, and organize all your sources. If you don't, you may even commit plagiarism accidentally. For example, you might find some phrases or sentences in your notes that perfectly express what you want to write at a particular point. But if you failed to note their source originally and just copy them, you would be copying someone else's work. It is not good enough just to change words around. If you want to use another person's material but not as a direct quote, you must paraphrase or summarize that material thoroughly and cite it properly.

How to avoid plagiarizing

Take and keep careful notes:

- As you take notes, always write down exactly where you read something.
- Keep your notes well organized, so that you can refer easily to original sources.

Give credit where it is due:

- Always cite where information comes from, especially if you are quoting it directly.
- Make full citations in any footnotes or endnotes and your bibliography.
- Even if you paraphrase information, consider writing, "As Joe Bloggs says, ...".
- Use quotation marks when something is a direct quote, so that this is clear.

Don't copy and paste:

- It is possible to copy and paste pieces of text from most websites. If you want to keep online sources, it is much better to print them rather than copying and pasting them into a word-processing document, so you remember they are someone else's work.
- Remember to paraphrase and summarize thoroughly. Never copy text directly unless it is a direct quote.

Prepare properly:

- Give yourself enough time to do your research and complete your report. If you are in too much of a rush, you might be tempted to take short cuts.
- Keep your notes and drafts of your report, so that if there is any doubt, you can show that your thoughts are your own.

Combating copying

Teachers, markers, and reviewers have many ways of finding out if work has been copied. Your teacher might instinctively sense that something has not been written by you – somehow it just doesn't seem right. The copied piece might be recognized, or several people might try to pass the piece off as their own. There are also special software programs that can find sources and identify copying. Even just typing a few words from a report into a search engine might achieve this.

Tips on making a spoken presentation

Read your report through several times out loud, so that you get used to any difficult words or passages and you always know what is coming next. This will make you sound more fluent and confident, and listeners will be impressed by your positive delivery. When reading your report, do your best to relax and breathe normally and deeply. Stand up straight and try to avoid moving around too much, such as shifting from one foot to the other or throwing your arms about. Look up from your report as often as possible, so that you communicate better with your audience.

Researching, writing, and presenting a report can be fun and interesting. Throughout the project you must be well organized and make sure it is all your own work.

It is essential that you speak loudly enough for everyone to hear you clearly. Speak in your natural voice and try to be as clear as possible, avoiding any mumbling. Emphasize the most important words and phrases. This emphasis is useful for understanding and helps to vary the pitch of your voice, which makes the presentation more interesting. Above all, try not to rush and deliver the whole thing too fast, which is what tends to happen if you are nervous. Take your time, and read your report clearly and confidently.

Research summary

Your research is made up of eight basic steps in this order:

1. *The overview*, in which you look at a broad outline of the Industrial Revolution and its main events.
2. *The basics*, finding out about different research tools and how to access them. These include books, the Internet, and graphic organizers.
3. *Digging deeper*, when you decide on a special topic and narrow the wider subject down to make it more manageable.
4. *Documents*, which you find and consult as the raw material of history, including primary sources that were written at the time and secondary sources that were written later.
5. *Images*, which can have just as much impact as words, but which you must look at critically.
6. *Other sources*, which you may find in libraries or using the Internet.
7. *Putting it all together*, the stage at which you assemble your evidence into a clear, well-organized form.
8. *The presentation*, in which you write your assignment in its final form and present it to others.

Glossary

alloy mixture that is a combination of more than one metal

apocryphal possibly untrue or of doubtful authorship

archive collection of documents on a subject or relating to a specific person, such as papers and photographs; also the name for the room or building that houses them

artefact object made by humans

atlas book of maps

bias presenting information in a way that supports a specific opinion

bibliography organized list of books and other sources referred to in a piece of research

caption text accompanying an illustration that describes its content

cite to quote something, such as a passage of text, as evidence for a statement

coke solid fuel made from coal

colony place in a different geographical area to a home country, but subject to its government and laws

concept web kind of graphic organizer that breaks a topic down and shows how sub-topics branch off and are related to each other

cottage industry small-scale business where goods are produced in the home

dust jacket paper cover wrapped around a book to protect it and which describes its contents

encyclopedia reference work in one or more volumes that contains information on a wide range of subjects; it may be printed or presented electronically or online

entrepreneur person who starts or manages a business and takes the financial risk as regards its success or failure

graphic organizer pictorial way of organizing information and presenting facts, such as charts and diagrams

italic printed in right sloping letters, *like this*

key words words that are most important to the understanding of a text; they might include names, dates, and locations

KWL chart chart presenting what you know, want to know, and learn in three columns

mass production goods produced in large numbers, especially in factories by machinery

non-fiction book book that presents factual information rather than a made-up story (which is called fiction)

online connected via a computer or other device to the Internet

paraphrase to reword or restate text in your own words

patent exclusive right given to a person to make and sell an invention

periodical magazine or journal published at regular intervals, such as weekly or monthly

plagiarism claiming someone else's work or ideas as your own; this is a form of cheating

primary source material produced by someone present at the time of an event

re-enactment acting out of a past event with as much accuracy as possible

reference mention of something, such as a source of information

reference book information book that can be used to find information on a subject

repeal cancel a law or government act

scan to look through a text quickly to find key words

search engine computer program that searches the Internet for key words and lists websites where they are found

secondary source material produced by someone after an event, usually referring back to primary sources

skim to read a text quickly to get an overall sense of its meaning and usefulness

small arms industry manufacturers of hand-held firearms

sporadically happening at irregular intervals

stock exchange place where people meet to buy and sell stocks and shares (financial units of interest in a business)

summarize to give a shortened version of something (a summary) by concentrating on the main points

telegraph form of long-distance communication that sends messages as electrical signals along wires

threshing machine machine used to remove the grains and seeds from harvested crops

URL web address, giving the location of a site on the Internet; short for Uniform Resource Locator

yarn spun thread of cotton or wool

Find Out More

Books

Some of the following books were written for adult readers, but they may be very useful to students.

Clare, John D. *I Was There: Industrial Revolution.* London: Bodley Head, 1993.

Connolly, Sean. *Witness to History: The Industrial Revolution.* Oxford: Heinemann Library, 2003.

Frader, Laura R. *Pages in History: The Industrial Revolution, A History in Documents.* Oxford: OUP, 2008.

MacDonald, Hamish. *From Workshop to Empire: Britain 1750–1900.* Cheltenham: Nelson Thorne, 1995.

Stearns, Peter N. *The Industrial Revolution in World History.* London: Westview Press, 2006.

Weightman, Gavin. *What the Industrial Revolution Did for Us.* London: BBC Books, 2003.

Williams, Brian. *History in Literature: The Story Behind Charles Dickens' Oliver Twist.* Oxford: Heinemann Library, 2007.

Websites

In addition to the websites mentioned throughout the book, the following are worth consulting:

www.bbc.co.uk/history/british/launch_tl_british.shtml
Explore periods of British history on an interactive timeline. When you click on an event, you get more detailed information. The sections relevant to the Industrial Revolution are Empire and Sea Power (1714–1837) and Victorian Britain (1837–1901).

www.spartacus.schoolnet.co.uk/IndustrialRevolution.htm
This educational website has a section on the Industrial Revolution with a wealth of links to many subsections.

Further research

The best way to learn how to research and access information is to practise doing it. Consider using the skills discussed in this book to research the following topics:

Is the Industrial Revolution over?

In *The Industrial Revolution in World History* (see page 54), the author breaks the Industrial Revolution down into three phases:

1) 1760–1880: The West leads the way
2) 1880–1950: The new international cast (especially Japan and Russia)
3) 1950–1990s: The industrialization of the world.

In the third phase, the author pays special attention to India, Israel, and China. You could look further into this question. Where in the world is the Industrial Revolution still taking place? Are the changes similar to those that occurred in the 18th and 19th centuries in Europe and North America?

The importance of oil

Oil has been an important source of energy, helping – along with coal – to fuel the Industrial Revolution in the United States and Russia, and making countries of the Middle East rich. Oil would make a good topic for research, and the history is interesting. Edwin Drake struck oil near Titusville, Pennsylvania, USA in 1859. Oil drilling and production along the Caspian Sea at Baku (in modern Azerbaijan) began in 1872. In the following year, Alfred Nobel, two of his brothers, and their friend Peter Bilderling founded the Nobel Oil Extracting Partnership in Baku. Alfred Nobel became a rich man from oil and dynamite, and established the Nobel prizes.

Agricultural, commercial, and electronic revolutions?

Was the Industrial Revolution really a revolution? What about the other three "revolutions": agricultural, commercial, and electronic? Beginning in the 17th century, great changes happened in European agriculture. Improved methods led to better yields, as leading farmers began treating agriculture as a science. How did this fit in with industry? In the 18th century, a system called mercantilism (dependent on colonies) was replaced by a capitalist system in which bankers, merchants, and industrialists became more important than landowners. The electronic revolution (which is still going on) came about in the late 20th century. What will be the next revolution?

Index